Making Pipes Is His Bag

written by Janet Cassidy

Table of Contents

Page

Inspiration

The Highland Bagpipe

Making a Bagpipe 11

Inspiration

Picture a rocky outcrop above a quiet cove, the beach covered with seaweed and driftwood. There a lone piper stands and plays. The sound of his instrument echoes in haunting strains across the water.

Many people consider the sound of a bagpipe wild, unforgettable, and deeply moving. Charley Kron first heard the sound of the Highland bagpipe band in California when he was five years old. "That started it all," he said, "I loved the sound." He never forgot that sound, or the interest in the instrument it kindled.

Little did he know that one day he would be a maker of bagpipes.

It was a long time before Charley had a chance to do anything about his interest in bagpipes, however. In the meantime, he learned to play two other reed instruments, the clarinet and the bassoon.

Then, when Charley was in college, he spent part of a semester in London, England. Because he was just a train ride away, he decided to spend the summer in Scotland. In the back of his mind was a desire to learn to play the bagpipes, Scotland's national instrument.

While he was in Edinburgh, Scotland's capital, he visited the company of J & R Glen, a world-renowned bagpipe maker. There he met George Stoddart, who agreed to teach him to play.

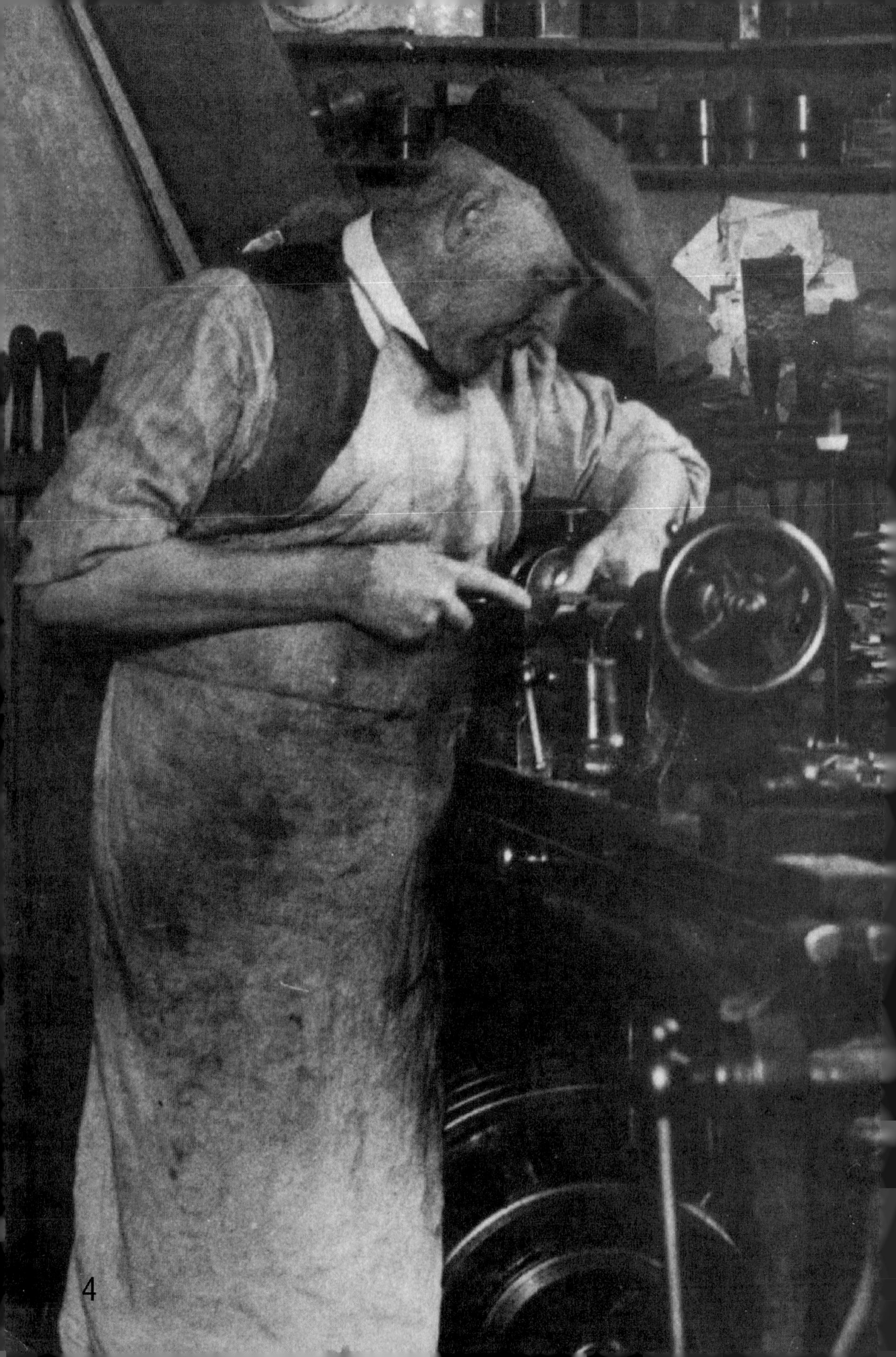

"I was already a musician, and I could read music," said Charley. "Also, I had little else to do, so I'd practice all day, eight hours a day! Practice, practice, practice! Of course I made fantastic progress."

The next summer, Charley returned to Scotland for more lessons. At the same time, he met another Scotsman, named George Kilgour. George worked for Robertson's, a well-known bagpipe maker's in Edinburgh. He made Charley his first set of pipes. Charley was fascinated by how the pipes were made. After college graduation in 1978, he went back to Scotland. He began to hang out in the shop all day, watching George make pipes. "I was fascinated by the old machines," said Charley.

Although Charley continued to improve as a piper, he soon became much more interested in making pipes than in playing them. Today, although certainly no disgrace as a player (he has won prizes in piping competitions), he has found his true calling as a custom maker of the instrument.

In the early 1980s, the shop where George Kilgour was working was sold. Eventually it went out of business. Charley and George decided to buy the machines and go into business for themselves.

Because the laws governing an American setting up business in Scotland were complicated, the two men decided to start their business in Dobbs Ferry, New York. Dobbs Ferry is a small town about thirty miles north of New York City, where Charley was then living. They opened in 1987.

It proved to be a good location. New York City is host to the world's largest St. Patrick's Day parade. It is also home to many people of Scottish and Irish descent, and to many others who love the bagpipes. In the New York metropolitan area there are more than fifty bagpipe bands.

The Highland Bagpipe

Bagpipes have been played throughout Europe for a thousand years or more. Almost every country has some form of bagpipe. The kind of bagpipe that is best known, however, is the Highland bagpipe.

A bagpipe consists of an airtight bag, usually of leather, and five pipes. One of these is the blowpipe, which the player uses to fill the bag with air.

Picking up a bagpipe to play has been compared to wrestling an octopus! In the hands of a novice, the instrument flails around a bit before being settled under the player's arm. Then the player inflates the bag with the blowpipe, squeezes the bag with the elbow, and forces the air out of the pipes.

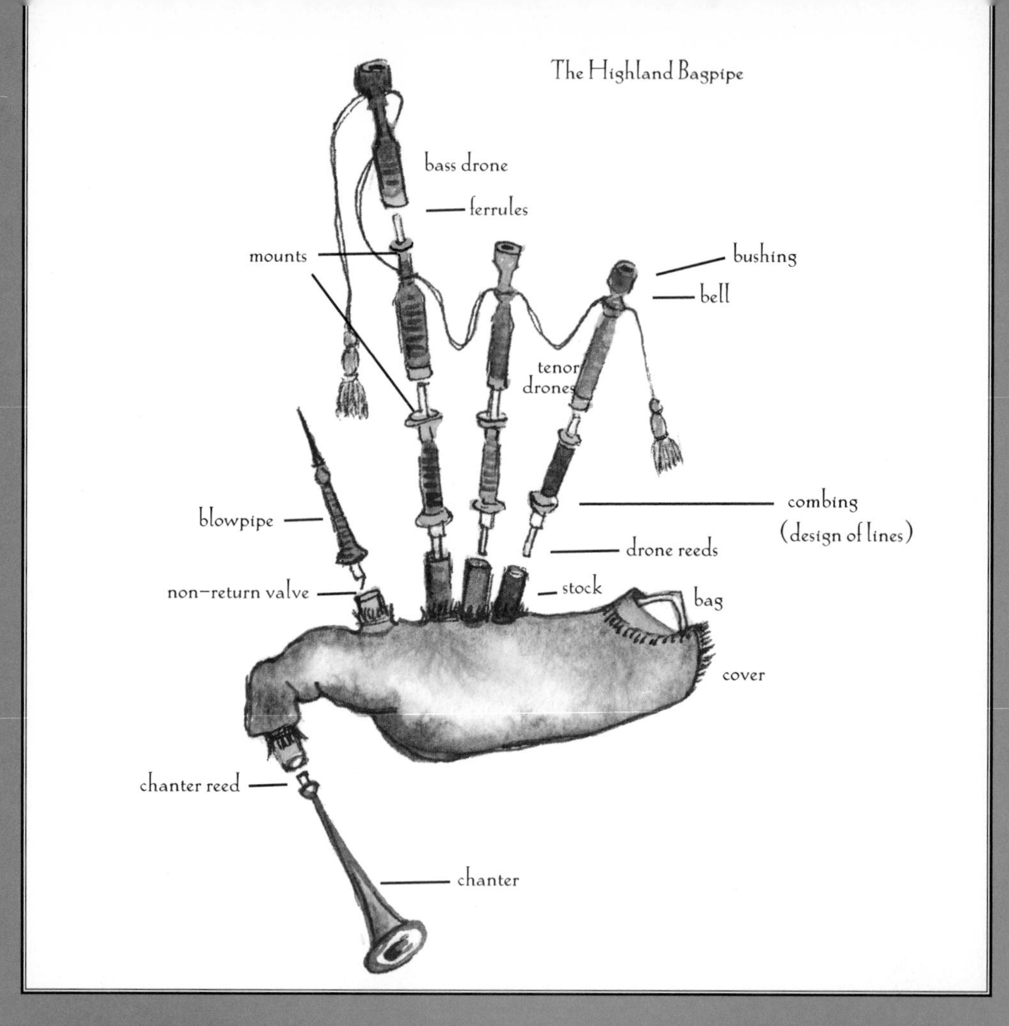

It takes practice to master squeezing the air out of the bag while blowing into it steadily to keep the bag filled. The whole time the pipes also have to be continually kept humming. With a good player, it is impossible to tell from the sound alone whether the player is blowing into the bag, or playing off the air already in the bag.

The three pipes that rest against the player's shoulder are called the *drones*. This is because they each play one note all the time, in a continuous humming, or droning, sound. The melody pipe is called the *chanter*. The player fingers it to play the tunes. The chanter contains a double reed, somewhat like an oboe reed.

The drones contain reeds, too, but of a different kind. Each is a pencil-shaped hollow reed about five inches long, with a single "tongue" that vibrates when air is forced through it. Traditionally, these reeds have been made of Spanish cane. In the past few years, reed makers have invented reeds that are a combination of cane and plastic. This has made setting up and playing the bagpipe much easier. Some players have even adopted all-plastic drone reeds.

The bagpipe is a very difficult instrument to play, but not because it is hard to blow. The reeds can be adjusted so a young child can blow into the instrument. However, in addition to the coordination needed to blow steadily, the fingering of the tunes is very tricky. The music uses many ornaments, which must be played exactly right.

Another reason the bagpipe is a difficult instrument is that it takes a lot of care to keep it in top playing at top condition. However, in the past ten years or so, technology has entered the bagpipe world! Inventions such as plastic drone reeds and a pipe bag made of synthetic fabric have made the piper's life easier.

One reason the bagpipe became famous in Scotland was because the Scots used it in battle. Pipers would play to inspire the soldiers, and to call the army together after the battle.

When Scotland became part of the United Kingdom, the British Army brought bagpipes into its Highland regiments. Wherever the British Army went, bagpipes went, too. The Highland bagpipe became known around the word, from the sands that sizzle in Egypt to the snows of Kilimanjaro. Today there are bagpipe players in India, Pakistan, Japan, Sudan, and Canada, as well as Ireland, Scotland, and the United States.

Making a Bagpipe

Each drone of the bagpipe is made of several sections. These come apart and can be moved to tune the pipes. In all, there are fourteen separate wooden sections in a bagpipe. Each must be made individually.

Charley uses African blackwood. This is an extremely thick, oily wood that comes from the east African countries of Mozambique and Tanzania. In the past, ebony and cocus wood were used to make pipes, too.

Charley buys blackwood from American wood dealers, who import it in solid blocks cut to size. The wood must be aged for several years to dry it before it can be used.

“If the block of wood is too heavy,” explains Charley, “it means it contains too much moisture and needs to be aged longer. If the wood isn’t dried enough, it will crack as it is being worked, or when the instrument is played.”

When the wood is ready, it is first “roughed down.” The corners of the block are knocked off, and the center is found. Each piece is examined carefully for flaws. The pieces that make up a bagpipe vary in length. If a block of wood has an imperfection at one end, it can often be used to make a different piece of the pipe. “The wood is too valuable to waste,” says Charley.

Next, the piece is bored out to make it hollow. To do this, the wood is clamped onto a lathe. This is a machine that holds the piece and turns it at a high rate of speed. In the old days, the pipemaker would use special hand-held bits of varying sizes. Each razor-sharp bit would be held against the spinning block of wood. Gradually, the inside of the wood would be bored out. In the past, it would take the maker about ten minutes to bore each piece. Today, using modern air drills, a piece is bored in about twenty seconds.

Then the top of the drone, known as the bell, is formed. The bell must be hollowed out carefully, because its shape is important to the sound of the drone. The piece is put on a lathe again, and shaped with other metal bits. Then the rest of the piece is shaped, giving it its outside contour.

The bell of each drone is fitted with a flat disc of artificial ivory called a *bushing*. This piece helps determine the sound of the drone. In the past, pipe makers used bone or elephant ivory to trim bagpipes. Since elephants have been placed on the endangered list, instrument makers have turned to artificial materials.

A special tool is then used to decorate the outside of each piece with a distinctive pattern of lines called *combing*. Then the mounts are attached. These are pieces of artificial ivory which are decorative, but which also help keep the wood of the drone from expanding and splitting.

The bores of the drones are the same diameter throughout. The shape is that of a cylinder. The chanter, or melody pipe, has a bore shaped like a cone that is narrower at the top and widens at the bottom. This gives the chanter more volume, but makes it more difficult to make than the cylindrical drones.

It takes about a week to make each set of pipes. Finally the pieces are finished. In the old days, pipemakers used shellac to varnish the pipes. Charley Kron uses a simple oil-based rubbed finish. Then the stocks are "tied in" to the leather bag, the drone cords are tied on, and the instrument is put together.

Charley and his assistant, Dave Atherton, make about a hundred sets of pipes a year. The pipes go to players across the United States.

For Charley, nothing beats turning the blocks of wood into a beautiful, hand-crafted instrument.

"There is nothing like the deep, rich sound of a well-made bagpipe," says Charley. "It's different from any other instrument."

"I love doing this," he adds. "It's the best job in the world."